TRAVEL GUIDE FOR QATAR:
A quick travel guide about Qatar's rich history and tourism amidst 2022 fifa world cup

Nellie A. Woods

TABLE OF CONTENTS

Introduction

There is evidence from recent discoveries that ancient people formerly resided in Qatar. Additionally, there is evidence that the ancient Qataris traded mostly in ceramics and dried fishes using barter systems. Both its kings and populace turned to Islam in the seventh century. Qatar actively participates in the Persian Gulf-Indian Ocean trade throughout the medieval era.

Because Qatar offers a fantastic viewpoint on their journey to their colony in India, the British decided to settle there. The Bahraini Al Khalifa tribe rules over the northern peninsula in the nineteenth century. The Al Khalifa family was revolted by the Qataris, who were then attacked by a sizable naval force. The British interfered, and a series of discussions followed even though the insurgents were vanquished. As a consequence, on December 18, 1878, the State of Qatar was established.

The Qataris choose businessman Muhammed bin Thani to represent them in negotiations with Bahrain and the British. His family, the Al Thani, would quickly ascend to power in Qatar.

When the British made their formal political withdrawal from the Persian Gulf known in 1968, Qatar formally joined a federation that also included Bahrain and seven other states. Qatar left the federation and proclaimed its independence on September 3, 1971, due to disagreements with it.

While on vacation in Switzerland in 1995, Hamad bin Khalifa Al Thani overthrew his father Khalifa bin Hamad Al Thani. The nation benefited from some sociopolitical liberalization under his tenure, including the freedom to vote.

Chapter 1:BRIEF HISTORY OF QATAR

It has been constantly but poorly populated from ancient times, taking up a tiny desert peninsula that stretches north from the wider Arabian Peninsula. The area was governed by the Islamic caliphate after the advent of Islam, and it then fell under the power of many local and foreign dynasties until being dominated by the Thani dynasty (l The) in the 19th century. The Ottoman Empire, which governed the nation in the late 19th and early 20th centuries, was fought out by the Thani family with British support. In return, the United Kingdom controlled Qatar's foreign policy until the latter's independence in 1971. After that, the monarchy maintained tight connections with Western nations as a key component of its national defense. Qatar has some of the greatest oil and gas reserves in the world, and a significant portion of its production is carried out by foreign labor. The nation's citizens benefit from a high level of living and a solid system of social services as a result of its oil resources.

The majority of the population lives in the eastern coastal city of Doha (Al-Dawah), which was historically a hub for pearling. Doha's attractive Corniche, or beachfront avenue, radiates inland and is ringed by new office buildings, shops, and housing complexes that combine premodern and modern design. From hand-woven goods to falconry, Qatari traditions are influenced by centuries-old customs and a nomadic history. The population is urban and coastal, everyday living is utterly contemporary, and the government has worked to strengthen civil freedoms. Although they are pious and traditional, Qataris take pride in their tolerance for other people's cultures and beliefs. The press is among the freest in the area. The country's sizable expatriate population, according to the reigning emir, "finds security and a respectable life in Qatar."

The Qatar peninsula is about 100 miles (160 km) long from north to south and 50 miles (80 km) wide from east to west. It has a little less area than the U.S. state of Connecticut and is mainly rectangular. It lies north and west of the United Arab Emirates and has a border with eastern Saudi Arabia where the peninsula joins the continent. Bahrain, an island nation, is located around 25 miles (40 km) northwest of Qatar. The International Court of Justice settled a territorial dispute with Bahrain in 2001 by awarding the war Islands (off the coast of Qatar) to Bahrain and granting Qatar sovereignty over Jann Island and the abandoned fortress town of Al-Zubrah (on the Qatari mainland). A definitive boundary delineation agreement between Qatar and Saudi Arabia was also inked in that year.

The majority of Qatar is made up of a low-lying, flat desert, which climbs in the east to a limestone plateau in the middle. The highest point in the nation is Ab al-Bawl Hill, which rises to a height of 335 feet (103 meters) on the western and northern beaches.

The main geographical characteristics of the southern and southeast sections are dunes and salt flats, or sabkhahs. The border between Qatar and Saudi Arabia is around 37 miles (60 km) long, and Qatar has more than 350 miles (560 km) of coastline. There are no permanent freshwater lakes or rivers. From June through September, the weather is hot and muggy, with daily highs around 122 °F (50 °C). The average temperature in the temperate spring and autumn months—April, May, October, and November—is about 63 °F (17 °C), whereas the winters are a little bit colder. The yearly amount of precipitation is less than 3 inches (75 mm) (generally in winter).

The majority of Qataris speak a Gulf Arabic dialect that is similar to that of the neighboring nations. Arabic is the official language of Qatar. In schools, Modern Standard Arabic is taught, while English is often spoken. Persian and Urdu are often spoken among the sizable expatriate community.

The majority of Muslims in Qatar are Sunni Muslims, and Islam is the national religion. A little Shi'i minority exists. Although not as firmly, the Thani dynasty, which now holds power, follows the same Wahhb interpretation of Islam as the monarchs of Saudi Arabia. For instance, Qatar offers women more freedom than Saudi Arabia. The religious composition of the non-Qatari population is more varied, with Muslims, Christians, and Hindus making up the bulk of the population.

Natural gas production and exports, which began in 1949 after petroleum was initially found there in 1939, are the main sources of Qatar's economic wealth.

With few exceptions, the only accessible jobs in pre-World War II Qatar were pearling, fishing, and minor trading, and the country's population was among the poorest in the world. The native population of Qatar, however, had one of the greatest per capita incomes in the world by the 1970s, despite later income decreases brought on by changes in global oil prices. An alliance of European and American companies, the Iraq Petroleum Company (IPC), was given the first oil concession by Qatar. The 1970s saw the nationalization of this concession as well as others.

While private enterprises continue to play a significant role as service providers, state-owned Qatar Petroleum (previously

Qatar General Petroleum Corporation) continues to control oil and gas activities.

.

Natural gas is abundant in Qatar, and its offshore North Field is one of the biggest gas resources in the whole globe. By regional standards, the nation's petroleum reserves, which are located both onshore at Dukhn along the western coast and offshore from the eastern coast, are minor.

Established in 1993, the Qatar Central Bank (Maraf Qaar al-Markaz) performs financial services for the government and issues the Qatari rial, the country's currency. Foreign banks with a license may operate alongside local banks, including commercial, development, and Islamic banks (organizations constrained by stringent religious laws controlling transactions). Qatar has been quite generous in its distribution of foreign assistance, especially to other Arab and Islamic nations. In 1997, the Doha Stock Exchange opened for business.

All citizens are entitled to free health care and medical services via government initiatives. As part of its comprehensive "youth welfare" effort, the government also provides funding for young people's access to clubs and facilities for leisure and culture. All inhabitants between the ages of 6 and 16 are entitled to free, albeit not mandated, education. Classes are divided based on gender.

Qatar has one of the highest per-pupil expenditures in the world and generously invests in education. Its network has significantly grown. Men's and women's teacher-training faculties were formed in 1973, and the group received university status in 1977 under the name University of Qatar. A second campus was built in Doha in 1985 as the institution continued to grow. The establishment of Education City, a multi-university campus outside of Doha, was motivated by a desire to make Qatar a significant regional research center. By the beginning of the twenty-first century, several American universities, including Virginia Commonwealth University, Weill Cornell Medical College (a division of Cornell University), Carnegie Mellon, Texas A&M University, Northwestern University, and Georgetown University, had branches in Education City.

The universities provided courses in business administration, journalism, fine arts, chemical, electrical, and mechanical engineering, as well as premedical and medical studies.

In addition, the government offers adult education courses in colleges and other institutions around the nation, with a focus on raising adult literacy. The literacy rate in the nation is around 4/5, with about equal numbers of boys and girls.

Fresh fish and rice prepared with Indian spices are staples of Qatari cuisine. A typical dinner can contain curry, potatoes, and grilled fish on a bed of seasoned rice. The preferred beverage is coffee, which is often served strong, very hot, and without sugar. There are several restaurants serving cuisines from all over the globe in Doha, the city's capital.

The two "ds," Eid al-Fitr and Eid al-Adha, as well as Ramadan, are all observed by the people of Qatar. They also observe several secular festivals, including the emir's coronation anniversary and Independence Day.

The Qatari Fine Arts Society and the few Doha-based galleries both support and show the work of regional artists. Literary, artistic, and cultural activities as well as leisure and tourism are governed by the National Council for Culture, Arts, and Heritage and several other organizations and ministries. Poetry, singing, and weaving—most often for carpets and pillows—is still done today by the Bedouin people. Although the Qatari government has made enormous attempts to preserve it, the nahmah (shanty) music genre that was formerly popular among pearl divers in Qatar and the larger Persian Gulf area has all but vanished.

The music of Arab, Pakistani, Indian, and other expatriate workers has influenced the nation, however, young people in Qatar prefer Western and Arab contemporary music over Bedouin or other traditional genres.

When a disagreement between the Qatari people and the Bahraini Khalifah—who still had some claim to Al-Zubrah—erupted into a massive clash in 1867, almost destroying Doha—the British became aware of Qatar. Before the incident, Britain had considered Qatar to be a Bahraini ally. The Thani dynasty's authority over Qatar was then established by a second contract that was made with Mohammed ibn Thani in 1868. Before this treaty, the Thani family had been only one of the numerous significant families on the peninsula.

Iraq Petroleum Company signed a concession deal. However, commercial oil recovery did not begin until 1949. The Qatar Petroleum Company, afterward known as Petroleum Development (Qatar) Limited, saw a sharp increase in its profits. The Thani family had severe internal strife over the allocation of these resources, which led the British to interfere in the 1949 succession and ultimately led to a palace coup in 1972 that installed Sheikh Khalifa ibn Hamad Al Thani as ruler.

The British government made preparations to leave the Gulf in 1968. On September 3, 1971, Qatar proclaimed its independence after discussions with the neighboring sheikhdoms that make up the modern United Arab Emirates (U.A.E.) and Bahrain.

A treaty of friendship took the role of past accords with Britain. Qatar joined the Arab League and the United Nations in the same month. The Gulf Cooperation Council (GCC), an alliance formed to foster economic cooperation and strengthen both internal security and external defense against the threats brought on by the Iranian Islamic Revolution and the Iran-Iraq War, was founded in 1981 when the emirate joined its five Arab Gulf neighbors.

Qatari forces took part in the 1990–1991 Persian Gulf War, particularly on January 30–31 in the conflict for control of the Saudi border town of Ras al–Khafj. The battle had little impact on Doha, which was used as a base for offensive airstrikes by French, Canadian, and American aircraft against Iraq and the Iraqi troops occupying Kuwait.

The 1995 palace revolution that installed Sheikh Hamad as ruler was also sparked by resurgent disputes about the sharing of oil profits. Khalifa opposed the coup even though his father had already allowed Hamad to take over day-to-day administration. Attempts at a countercoup in 1996 and a lengthy legal dispute with his father over who should be entitled to billions of dollars in invested oil income had to be overcome by Hamad before he could completely consolidate his authority. The latter dispute was ultimately resolved out of court.

In the 1990s, Qatar agreed to allow American military personnel to set up equipment at various locations all around the nation and allowed them to use Qatari airstrips in 2001 for American operations in Afghanistan. These arrangements were confirmed in late 2002, and the following year Qatar was chosen as the base for American and allies' military operations in Iraq.

In the first decade of the twenty-first century, rising natural gas demand helped Qatar's economy reach new heights and funded its ambitions to advance from relative obscurity to a position of greater significance in the Middle East.

The government of Qatar made significant investments in development, paying particular attention to famous cultural initiatives like museums and satellite campuses for international institutions. By supporting Al Jazeera, a well-liked satellite television network recognized for its generally independent news coverage, which often featured criticism of autocratic Arab regimes and U.S. Middle East policy, Qatar also attempted to establish a reputation for openness and political independence. Although Qatar continued to be an absolute monarchy and to be home to a sizable U.S. military post, criticism of the nation was conspicuously missing from the network's broadcasts.

Being friendly with a wide range of Middle Eastern nations and organizations was a defining feature of Qatar's foreign policy, which occasionally required striking a balance between rival regional nations like Iran and Saudi Arabia or between secular governments and Islamist opposition groups like the Muslim Brotherhood. With a reputation for objectivity, Qatar looked for chances to improve its international status by mediating conflicts in the Middle East.

These efforts had varying degrees of success: in 2007, a deal Qatar brokered between the Yemeni government and the Houthi rebels disintegrated within months, but in 2008, Qatar played a key role in ending a standoff between rival factions in Lebanon that had the potential to escalate into an armed conflict.

Political overview of qatar

In Qatar, there are no political parties. The first parliamentary election was conducted in 2021, while Qataris have been able to cast ballots in municipal elections since 1999. Citizens who are 18 years of age or older and whose paternal grandfather was born in the nation are only permitted to vote. Female candidates for public office are accepted.

Qatar is a constitutional emirate with a single advisory body and is headed by an emir who is descended from the 1 The. Nearly all of the important cabinet positions are held by members of the royal family and are chosen by the emir. However, the family is big and dispersed. After World War II, as oil profits increased, tensions within the royal family developed, and there have been several non-violent palace coups.

The necessity to keep the support of significant family members, many of whom hold crucial government positions, limits the emir's influence. The political stability of Qatar is influenced by the homogeneity of the ruling family and the riches of the nation.

The emir has also gradually increased political engagement, allowing the first municipal elections to be held in 1999 with both male and female Qataris participating in the voting process. An interim constitution adopted in 1972 stated that the emir had the support of both an appointed Advisory Council (Majlis al-Shr) and a Council of Ministers (Majlis al-Wuzar).

A new constitution that was adopted in 2005 and ratified by referendum in 2003 called for the election of two-thirds of the Advisory Council's members.

Chapter 2:FUN FACTS ABOUT QATAR

Qatar, one of the smallest but most powerful nations in the Persian Gulf, is a place with a lot of fascinating information and entertaining things to do. It is one of the richest nations on earth and will host the FIFA World Cup in 2022 for the first time in an Arab nation.

You will discover some extremely intriguing facts about Qatar below, from the background of the country's flag to a huge teddy bear kept at the major international airport. These Qatari facts may maybe pique your interest to the point where you consider traveling there soon.

Fun facts about QATAR include

The world's safest nation is Qatar.

The national dish of Qatar is machboos.
The world's top airline is Qatar Airways.
The inhabitant of Hamad International Airport is a huge bear.
The third-best airport in the world is Hamad International Airport.
In Qatar, there are no woods.
Where the sea meets the desert, Qatar is the second-most flat nation in the world.
As the first country to produce purple shrimp dye, Qatar will be the first Arab nation to host the FIFA World Cup.
The Arabian Oryx is an emblematic animal.
Gas in Qatar is relatively affordable.
The world's longest oil well is located there.
The flag of Qatar is quite distinctive and significant.
In Qatar, males outweigh women three to one.

Qataris make up only 12% of the population. The capital city of Qatar, Doha, is home to 99% of the country's citizens.

No central core exists in the Doha Tower.

The nation's name first appeared around 50 AD.

National Day in Qatar wasn't always observed on the same day.

Saturdays and Fridays are the weekend days.

There is a falcon obsession in Doha, which boasts the world's longest continuous cycling route.

A gorgeous pearl thread runs across Qatar.

Since 1868, the ruling family has been in control. They like using robots for camel racing.

A 100-meter-long buffet offers unlimited food.

Many properties in London, England, are owned by Qatar.

Chapter 3: TOURIST ATTRACTIONS IN QATAR

Museum of Islamic Art:
A Beautiful Building
The Museum of Islamic Art, an architectural marvel located in the MIA Park on the Doha waterfront, is regarded as one of the city's most popular tourist destinations. The Museum of Islamic Art is one museum that houses the biggest collection of Islamic art on the whole globe. It was designed by the famous architect I.M. Pei. While the paintings were amassed over 1400 years from three continents, the interiors are gorgeous and include stunning geometric designs from the Islamic world, making it one of the numerous attractions in Doha to

visit at night. Undoubtedly, it is a well-known Doha tourist destination.
The place is Doha, Qatar.
Hours are 9 AM to 7 PM.
No admission fee. Price
Has the biggest collection of Islamic art in the world.

2. Corniche: Leisure Activities
The Doha Corniche is among Qatar's top tourist destinations. The Corniche is a waterfront promenade that altered Doha's shoreline in the late 1970s and early 1980s. It is one of the most well-liked sites among walkers, cyclists, and runners. In addition to being a great location for morning exercise, it draws large people in the evening to observe breathtaking sunsets and enjoy breathtaking views of the city skyline.
The place is Doha, Qatar.
Timings: Always open.
No admission fee. Price
Reputation: Stunning views of the city

3. Souq Waqif: The Love of a Shopaholic
Considering a tour of Doha city? If the answer is yes, you should not miss out on going to the Souq Waqif, which serves as a one-stop location for eating and shopping. One may stroll around the lanes, marvel at the architecture, shop for spices, fragrances, oud (a unique incense produced from agarwood), and more at this popular Doha site.

 This is one of the greatest spots to visit in Doha near the airport if you have a stopover in Qatar.

Location: Doha, Qatar's Aspire Park Running Trail

10 a.m. to 12 p.m. and 4:30 p.m. to 10 p.m.

No admission fee. Price

Known For: Purchasing souvenirs, dining, and scents

4:Khalifa International Tennis and Squash Stadium

There are several attractions in Doha, including the Khalifa International Tennis and Squash Stadium, which keeps tourists occupied and amused by providing a variety of recreational activities. This stadium, which has 21 tennis courts, is the greatest a sports enthusiast could find.

In Al Dafna, Doha, Qatar, on Al Majles Twain Street

Time: Opens at 10 a.m.

5. Serene Views at Aspire Park

Aspire Park, one of the Gulf's biggest parks and one of Qatar's most beautiful landscapes, is regarded as one of the best locations to visit in Qatar with family. The Torch Tower often referred to as the Aspire Tower, is another feature of the park. The towering 300-meter-high structure, which functioned as a massive torch during the 15th Asian Games and is now a stunning hotel, is amazing. It is one of the most popular sites to visit in Qatar during the summer, so be sure to include it in your itinerary when making travel plans.

Location: Doha, Qatar's Aspire Park Running Trail

8:00 a.m. to 12:00 a.m.

No admission fee. Price

Known for: Beautiful landscapes

6. Enjoy the Events at Katara Cultural Village

The renowned Katara Cultural Village, one of the top sites to visit in Doha, is situated on the eastern shore between West Bay and The Pearl. Huge occasions like the TEDx Doha, the Ajyal Youth Film Festival, and the Doha Tribeca Film Festival are held there. The structures and amenities of the cultural hamlet have been set up to resemble a typical Al Faraj in Qatar.

The place is Doha, Qatar.

Open 24 hours a day

No admission fee. Price

Known For: Hosting several events

7;The Pearl: A Man-Made Island

The Pearl, an artificial island off the coast of Doha's West Bay Lagoon, is well-known for being the first piece of property in Qatar to be open to foreigners for freehold ownership. Tourists come here to browse the area's many high-end retail stores or just to stroll along the lovely promenade that overlooks the harbor. It is one of the most well-liked tourist destinations in Doha.

Location: Doha, Qatar (7256)

Hours: 10 a.m. to 10 p.m.

No admission fee. Price

Famous For: Being the first piece of property in Qatar that foreigners could purchase the freehold.

8. Impressive Artifacts in the Qatar National Museum

The second-largest museum in Doha, the Qatar National Museum, offers visitors an excellent selection of antiquities and artifacts. This renowned museum, one of the most well-known attractions in Doha, is a beautiful illustration of Arabian culture and was given the Agha Khan Award for the restoration of Islamic architecture in 1980. A must-see sight, one may take in a variety of exhibits that are scheduled throughout the year. One of the top tourist destinations in Doha is this.

Location: Doha, Qatar, Museum Park St.

Hours are 9 AM to 7 PM.

Adults pay INR 1000 approximately.

Known For: Preserves the history of the little country in the Arabian Gulf

9. Apprise Your Soul: Islamic Cultural Center (FANAR)

A well-known tourist destination in Doha is the Islamic Cultural Center, or Fanar, which is housed within the spiral mosque next to Souq Waqif. This cultural center serves as a nonprofit with the mission of educating non-Muslims about Islam and its culture via a variety of events including exhibits, tours of the facility, and even Arabic classes. Fanar, one of the best destinations in Qatar for families, is adjacent to Souq Waqif and the Museum of Islamic Art, both of which you may visit in addition to FANAR.

The place is Doha, Qatar.

Hours: Monday through Thursday, 7:15 AM to 1:15 PM; Friday and Saturday closed

Price: Free admission

Famous For: communal, spiritual, and educational pursuits

10: Sealine Beach Resort: A Calm Haven

The Sealine Beach Resort is regarded as one of the best locations to visit in Qatar during the summer. This resort, an oasis of peace, is situated by the clear waves of the Arabian Sea among the dunes of the Arabian Desert. Aside from enjoying a sumptuous stay, guests may experience dune bashing, which is still a popular pastime among locals and visitors alike, by renting a dune buggy on the beach next to the resort. Having said that, this is among the top tourist destinations in Doha.

Location: Mesaieed, Qatar, along Sealine Beach Road

Timings: Always open.

Price: Starting at INR 2500

Known for: its serene ambiance and opulent facilities

11. Heightened Views from Barzan Towers

The Barzan towers are watchtowers, and they are situated on the southern flank of the defense system. The 16-meter-high tower was specifically designed to watch out for ships approaching the city. In addition to this, the tower has two additional structures: one on its western and one on its northern side. It is a must-see site in Doha for everyone who likes heights.

Location: Qatar, Mohammed

Timings: Always open.

No admission fee. Price
Heightened vistas of the area are well
known.

Accommodations options

With its wide selection of hotels and
well-known hospitality, Qatar offers
something for everyone. While the majority
of hotels are found in Doha, the country's
capital, there are also several outlying
getaways for those seeking something
different.

favorite places to stay
Downtown Doha is a place where old and
modern coexist together. If you want to fully
experience Doha's rich Arabic traditions and
contemporary architecture, this is the place
to stay. There are several hotels available
here, ranging in price from luxury to budget.

Al Sadd is a neighborhood popular with ex-pat families that is located just west of the ancient city of Doha. You may discover affordable lodging, high-end stores, boutiques, and restaurants from practically anywhere in the globe here.

The famous cityscape of Qatar is seen at West Bay, where contemporary buildings are artfully arranged along the Corniche. The majority of lodging is upscale and elegant, ideally placed close to shopping, recreation, and entertainment.

Some of Qatar's best hotels and upscale lodging may be found in The Pearl-Qatar, which also includes the adjacent Lagoona. Six marinas, gorgeous beaches, exquisite eating, and designer outlet stores are all available in the vicinity.

What to anticipate:
3- to 5-star inns (mid-range to premium luxury)
2 and 1-star hotels

both small local establishments and global hotel chains
Arabic tradition and well-known worldwide brands
locations on a beach, in a suburb, in the city, or on islands and lagoons
Excellent services and hospitality

Qatar redefines hospitality and offers a variety of resorts to suit every demand. Witness opulent rooms and suites, take use of first-rate recreational amenities and go on incredible gastronomic journeys while admiring picturesque views and learning about the local way of life.

Al Messila Resort & Spa
Al Messila, a Luxury Collection Resort & Spa, Doha, invites visitors to spend their days immersed in a lavish sanctuary. It is tucked between the desert and the bustling city center. Al Messila Resort & Spa is a paradise for visitors with rooms and suites that meet all demands and provide a

genuine sense of home, a distinctive Al Messila Spa that offers a fresh viewpoint on holistic health, and restaurants that will tantalize your taste buds.

Mandarin Oriental, Doha
At the center of Barahat Msheireb, the city's newest and most dynamic neighborhood, the Mandarin Oriental, Doha is an intimate and fashionable urban getaway.

Banyan Tree Doha at La Cigale Mushaireb
Banyan Tree Doha is an urban luxury resort in Doha that redefines elegance, comfort, and hospitality. It is situated in the center of Mushaireb. Banyan Tree Doha provides a peaceful refuge to revitalize the mind, body, and soul in an inspiring ambiance, enabling visitors to savor the warm hospitality while creating real-world experiences that stick in their minds.

Anantara's Banana Island Resort in Doha
The first and only overwater villas in Qatar are available to visitors at Banana Island Resort Doha by Anantara, giving them a taste of traditional Qatari hospitality.

City Centre Rotana Doha hot
The City Centre Rotana Doha Hotel is well situated in Doha's West Bay neighborhood, making it the perfect luxury accommodation choice for tourists and business travelers who wish to remain near the city's center.

The St. Regis Doha
St.Regis goes above and beyond to welcome and amuse visitors. It is situated in the West Bay, the center of commerce in Doha, and near one of the city's most picturesque neighborhoods, the Pearl. The resort will undoubtedly be remembered for its tailored

luxury services, personalized amenities, diverse culinary selections that go above and above, and recreational facilities that provide the ideal retreat for the whole family.

La Cigale Hotel Managed by Accor
A high-design hotel with a 20-story façade, La Cigale Hotel provides guests with a luxury lodging choice that is brimming with Qatari hospitality. La Cigale Hotel, located in the center of the city, is happy to offer 225 opulent rooms and suites, 9 exquisitely designed dining and entertainment venues with outdoor sitting spaces, and more. The building is particularly well-known for its two renowned contemporary ballrooms, Al Wajba and Le Crillon, as well as its popular nightlife venue, the Sky View.

The Ritz-Carlton, Doha
The Ritz-Carlton, Doha, which has been reimagined to represent a new era in its

tradition, honors the innovative spirit of the city with an elite Club level, distinctive dining choices, opulent rooms, signature suites, a one-of-a-kind spa adventure, and iconic outdoor and indoor pools. This five-star city resort blends the past and the present to provide a diverse, multicultural experience that is distinguished by outstanding elegance. Its distinguishing features include the biggest chandelier in the Middle East.

The Ritz-Carlton Sharq Village Doha

The Ritz-Carlton Spa Sharq Hamlet, Doha, is a beachfront facility that was inspired by a traditional Qatari village. It offers magnificent accommodation and spa experiences that will stimulate your senses. The hotel's 174 rooms and suites, many of which have their courtyard settings, represent the rich history and traditions of Qatar that date back many centuries.

AlRayyan Hotel Doha, a Hilton Curio Collection

The AlRayyan Hotel Doha, Curio Collection by Hilton, conveniently located in the Mall of Qatar's retail area, continues to work its magic with a spectacular new offering that is sure to be another magnet for families traveling to Qatar.

Salwa Hilton Beach Resort

With a range of amenities, the Hilton Salwa Beach Resort & Villas offers opulent, sumptuous, and peaceful lodging choices. Top-notch water and adventure park, spas, swimming pools, a sports club, a variety of upscale restaurants, exhilarating activities, and much more can be found at this family-friendly resort.

W Doha

Where casual glitz meets urban vitality is at W Doha. The building is renowned for its grandeur, service, amenities, and modern dining scenes. 240 bedrooms, 51 suites, and

153 W branded homes are available at the hotel, each with a distinctive design.

Zubarah Boutique Hotel

The contemporary boutique hotel Zubarah Hotel, which offers genuine Qatari hospitality and integrates seamlessly into Doha's urban scene, guarantees guests an unparalleled level of service and a customized way of life.

Modarin Doha

Where the city comes alive is at Mondrian Doha. The hotel is situated in West Bay at the intersection of Doha and Lusail City and was built to accommodate all types of travelers. The Mondrian Doha is a famous hotel that epitomizes elegance, exquisite design, and a dash of regional flavor.

Golden Tulip, Doha

Offering the finest of both Old and New Doha is the Golden Tulip Doha Hotel. Golden Tulip Doha offers accommodations for both short- and long-term stays has an excellent location, and caters to experienced travelers.

Cielo Lusail, hotel
Visit the Cielo Lusail Hotel to experience unmatched elegance and first-class hospitality. Its central position in Lusail City, proximity to Place Vendome Mall and The Pearl, Lusail University, Qetaifan Island, Marina Lusail, and its short commute to Hamad International Airport make it readily accessible to anyone.

Accommodations for visitors to the FIFA World Cup

Various lodging choices are available in Qatar during the 2022 World Cup, including hotel rooms (ranging in star quality from 2 to 5),

floating hotels, and fan communities.

The first lodging choice is hotels (ranging in star rating from two to five), which is the standard option for lodging during different events, whether they are sporting or not. The majority of Qatar's hotels are in the capital city of Doha, which offers a large variety of hotels and other lodging options, although there are numerous locations outside the city for travelers seeking something different.

The price of a room per night in two- and one-star hotels has been established by the Qatari Ministry of Commerce and Industry at 296 Qatari riyals ($81), in three-star hotels at 438 riyals ($120), and conventional four-star hotels at 482 riyals ($132). And a premium 4-star room costs 886 riyals ($242.74).

For 5-star accommodations, the maximum per-night rate was set at 911 riyals ($343.77) for regular lodging, 1488 riyals ($407.67) for premium lodging, 2,133 riyals ($584.38) for luxury lodging, and up to 2801 riyals ($767.39) for 5-star independent resort lodging.

Floating hotels/ inns

The second lodging choice is one of the floating hotels along Qatar's coast. A first in the history of the World Cup, which will be played for the first time in the Middle East and the Arab globe, it will be a thrilling experience for supporters from all over the world to take in a spectacular vista overlooking the Arabian Gulf.

Cruise ships are one of the sustainable housing alternatives for the Qatar World Cup, thus the Supreme Committee for Delivery and Legacy struck a deal with MSC Cruise Ships to charter two cruise ships that will be utilized as floating hotels and have a capacity of roughly 4,000 rooms.

Both floating hotels provide a selection of accommodation types, including classic cabins with sea views, rooms with balconies, and opulent suites.

- Hotel on a cruise ship, Poesia
Fans of the World Cup will have a unique lodging opportunity thanks to the floating hotel, which offers a range of accommodations, from suites and balconies to inside cabins with bay views.

The cost of a hotel room per night is around 640 riyals, which is $179.34.

Hotel World Europa cruise ship

Fans of the FIFA World Cup in Qatar can enjoy unmatched architecture and technology, as well as a broad variety of lodging alternatives, including opulent suites with exquisite private facilities and cozy traditional cabins, as well as a spectacular outdoor promenade.

Fan villages

The Fan Villages, which will include a variety of conventional camping sites and lodging cabins and promise fans unique adventures and a festive atmosphere while watching the event, will be the other option for lodging for the 2022 World Cup visitors. These accommodations will mimic living in a festival for visitors.

The most well-known fan villages during the World Cup will be those near the Sealine resort, which can accommodate 2,000 supporters who will live in Arab tents, providing tourists with a unique opportunity to see a variety of cultures.

Chapter 4:SPECIAL QATAR'S CULINARY CUISINE

If you ask a gourmet this question, food will be their response. Qatar, one of the best Middle Eastern nations, is undoubtedly gastronomic heaven. Food has played a significant role in Qatari culture and serves as a unifying force among its people. Food is always a hot topic, whether it's during celebrations, social gatherings, or any other type of event. In reality, as far as traditional cuisine is concerned, Qatar has a lot to offer.

Today, the nation is home to a variety of top-notch eateries that have established themselves in part due to the traditional cuisine they serve. So let's examine some of Qatar's best traditional foods in further detail.
Machboos

Machboos, a spicy rice meal that may be made by marinating chicken, beef, lamb, camel, or even fish, is perhaps the greatest cuisine in Qatar and is deeply ingrained in the minds of locals. Since Machboos is the national food of Qatar, it is simple to find it there since every restaurant serves it in some form.

Thanks to the dish's lengthy cooking time, Machboos is a superb taste combination for connoisseurs of fine cuisine.

If you're visiting Qatar, you really must taste this meal. But hold on, do you know what makes Machboos interesting? In Qatar, every restaurant serves a unique blend of Machboos. Other places place a greater emphasis on delivering the most genuine flavor, while others offer it in their unique style. The Souq Waqif neighborhood in Doha is home to several quaint eateries that offer Machboos in their original taste.

Saloona

Saloona has a long history in Qatari cuisine. Almost any kind of item that is on hand may be used to make this recipe. The majority of the restaurants in Doha provide Saloona, which is quite well-liked in Qatar. This is one meal that is served during family gatherings in Qatar, and the scent of the meat, fish, or lamb combined with ginger and garlic makes it even more remarkable.

Tomatoes, aubergines, carrots, and potatoes are among the other components in Saloona. The meal is often served with broth in the capital of Qatar's eateries, which is the best way to eat it.

Want to know where you can sample it? Saloona is available in a lot of the best restaurants in the nation. Restaurants in places like Souq Waqif or even Pearl Qatar provide this well-known dish from Qatar. In Souq Waqif, several eateries offer saloona in its original flavor. Visit any traditional restaurant in Doha to sample the famous Saloona meal.

Luqaimat

Luqaimat is another renowned traditional dish in Qatar that is enjoyed across the whole nation. During the holy month of Ramadan, when friends and family join together for a night of dessert-filled fun, this meal is often offered. Luqaimat is a dish that resembles a dumpling in many ways. It is made using butter, milk, flour, sugar, saffron, and cardamom.

The dumplings are cooked in oil and then dipped in honey or sugar syrup. What follows is a feast full of sweetness and many tastes. This meal will delight your tooth since it has a crispy outside and a soft inside.

Customers may now find Luqaimat at a lot of Qatari restaurants that specialize in serving traditional cuisine. In fact, during the holy month of Ramadan, almost every home in Qatar prepares this delicacy. So why not give Luqaimat a try at any Qatari restaurant?

Warak Enab
Warak Enab is a classic Qatari cuisine that may be enjoyed at any time of day. It is also one of the greatest Qatari foods to try as a snack. This is a tasty light snack that is packed with various components and is very well-liked by tourists. A variety of eateries and little cafés can be found at Souq Waqif, one of the most well-liked tourist destinations in Qatar, where Warak Enab is served in its purest form.

The meal, which is sometimes referred to as filled grape leaves, is made with rice, herbs, tomatoes, salt, pepper, and a variety of other ingredients. Instead of rice, the leaves may instead be filled with ground beef or lamb.
It's interesting to note that you may request specific preparations for this popular Qatari dish. So, if you're vacationing in Qatar, be

sure to sample Warak Enab at one of the nation's genuine restaurants.

Khanfaroush in Saudi

Have you ever heard of the ideal marriage of cake and biscuits? That's Khanfaroush for you, then. This is a fried sweet that is presented in the shape of a disc and is another well-liked traditional dish in Qatar. This dish is a must-try for tourists visiting Doha and other regions of Qatar. Khanfaroush is a deep-fried delicacy similar to various other sweets offered in the nation. It is served with either sugar or a thin layer of honey, which enhances the flavor of the meal.

But wait—do you know what Khanfaroush's finest feature is? This delicacy has a crisp exterior and, thanks to the use of rosewater in the preparation process, a flowery scent that is nothing short of dreamy for a gourmet. What's best? It improved the dish's flavor as well.

What is the delay, then? Taste Khanfaroush at any restaurant. If you're fortunate, you could even get to sample it in a local's home.

Baleelat

Are you a gastronome who enjoys experimenting with various cuisines or a picky eater who prefers just certain flavors? In any case, you owe it to yourself to treat yourself to some of the best Qatari food. Through its kindness, openness, and hospitality, Qatar blends its rich tradition and culture. Since its flavors, tastes, and distinctiveness are a part of its legacy, its cuisine is comparable. Baleelat is a popular traditional Qatari breakfast that draws tourists from all over the globe. It is often offered as a dessert that exemplifies the delicious cuisine's variety.

The meal, which may be served hot or cold, may seem unusual at first, but the moment you take a mouthful, the tastes explode in your mouth, bounce off your tongue, and provide a spectacular flavor you've never experienced before. People will continually return for more. What are you waiting for if you haven't already given it a try? You are unaware of what you are missing.

Madrouba

The traditional dish of Madrouba, a rice porridge, is a culinary delight in Qatar. The meal takes hours to prepare since it is boiled until the chicken, milk, butter, and cardamom are all mushy. Every restaurant in Qatar prepares food differently. People are often advised to study up on the meal before eating it since the toppings may vary in certain circumstances.

During the day, one may consume the savory meal madrouba. The Souq Al Wakrah's labyrinth of courtyards and lanes is the perfect location to consume the meal.

At Café Easir, a variety of delicious Qatari appetizers are provided along with this scrumptious chicken meal.

Kousa Mahshi
One of the most magnificent Middle Eastern dishes, kousa mahshi is cooked with minced lamb, vegetables, parsley, and mint. It is one of several vegetarian recipes made using chickpeas rather than lamb. With tomato paste or yogurt, the flavors of the meal are enhanced even more. One might visit Salwa RD in Doha if they are in the mood for this Middle Eastern meal. People can enjoy a one-of-a-kind experience at Al Shami Home Restaurant.

The eatery is well-known for its authentic Berber tent, which has a marble fountain and cloth hanging from the ceiling. It comes in huge servings and is flavored in a variety of ways. What are you still waiting for? Give your tastebuds a taste of Middle Eastern cuisine's greatest dishes.

Umm Ali

Have you ever experienced one of the Middle East's most delectable desserts? Umm Ali, one of the best sweets, is associated with Egypt, although the Middle East has its unique method of preparation. Umm Ali, the sweetest dessert in Qatar, is made with raisins, chopped nuts, and condensed milk. It is then baked until it is golden and crispy on top.

Karaki, a sweet Karak tea, and sweets and pastries have helped Umm Ali establish a reputation. The mouthwatering creamy filling contains dried fruit and a variety of spices. When it comes to treating their tongue to one of the most genuine desserts, what more could anybody ask for? For most people, having such a meal all day long has been a dream come true.

Cheese and Kunafa

Do you like eating any meal that comes your way, regardless of how sweet it may be? One of the most popular Middle Eastern desserts, kunafa with cheese causes people to salivate and hanker for more after just one bite. It has ascended to the top of Doha's Qatari cuisine with certain taste additions. It is among the dishes that are often consumed during Ramadan. People will be brought to paradise or, more accurately, taken on a voyage through the land of the sweets when they think of biting into something that is covered in sugar and melted cheese. Isn't it too wonderful to be true?

Every year, people may treat themselves to delicious confection. One of the venues in Doha where people may treat themselves to a Kunafa is Al Aker Sweets, which is tucked away amid Souq Waqif. If you're yearning for more sweetness, Nutella Kunafa is the perfect solution. People will never want to leave the Middle East since there is so much diversity there.

Thareed

There are many mouthwatering foods in the Middle East that foreigners and tourists may not be familiar with. However, here is where Qatar's beauty began. The cuisine must be enjoyed here since it embodies the warmth and cultural traditions of the nation. One of the most traditional dishes available in Qatar is thareed. Thareed is made out of a mixture of vegetables, roots, and meat from different animals, much like a pot of stew. This well-known meal from Qatar is often served with bread, which is claimed to soak up all the liquids and provide a mouthful. Although this meal is often referred to be lasagna made in Qatar.

Qatar Street Food:

Any gourmet would say "everything" when asked what street food meant to them. In Qatar, street food is a major factor in enhancing your experience of the country's busy streets. Qatar boasts a wide variety of street food, including the greatest traditional snacks as well as rolls and wafers.

Here are some of the most well-known street snacks you may discover in Qatar if you plan to visit any well-known tourist destinations in Doha or elsewhere.

Shawarma
Shawarma is a dish that everyone is familiar with. Shawarma is one of the most well-liked street snacks worldwide, not only in Qatar. Shawarma is freely accessible on the streets of Doha. This delicacy is made with stacked, grilled boneless slices of beef or chicken that are placed on a spinning skewer. The margins of the meat are cut into slices and wrapped in bread while it gently cooks. Typically, shawarma is served with pickles, sauce, and fries. However, it's noteworthy to notice that each restaurant or

street food stand uniquely makes Shawarma.

Falafel

Falafel is another well-liked street cuisine that tourists may sample in Doha. This is a well-liked vegan snack that is offered as flat cutlets or crunchy deep-fried balls. This is often a go-to snack for those who eat vegan food. Ground chickpeas, fava beans, and sometimes even both are used to make falafel. Tahini, coriander, and other ingredients are combined with it to enhance the taste.

Samboosa

Have you ever had an Indian samosa? Try Qatar's delectable samboosa right now. Samboosa, a delicacy that may be found in both Chinese and African cuisines, is sometimes referred to be the contemporary equivalent of filled fried dumplings. Samboosa is significantly smaller and is served with a thin crust, in contrast to samosa, which is larger and has a potato filling in South Asia.

Samboosa is a popular street snack in Qatar and is available at some of the best restaurants there. This well-known dish from Qatar is packed with cheese, spinach, or even minced beef. The meal is also accompanied by a variety of chutneys, each with a distinctive taste.What about the Indian version, however, and how does it compare to Samboosa? In terms of appearance, Samosa and Samboosa are identical. Smaller versions of samosas with chicken or cheese filling are now available in India as well.

Pani Puri
Pani Puri may be found anywhere, from the busy streets of Doha to Bombay Chowpatty. Pani Puri is a popular dish in Doha that originates from the streets of India. It resembles a hollow ball that is filled with a

variety of ingredients. Potatoes, onions, and chickpeas are a few of the main components of pani puri. Restaurants, however, serve in their manner using various components.

The delicious flavor of Pani Puri is what draws tourists there. What truly enhances the overall flavor of the snack is the flavored water that is used with it. In addition, Pani Puri may be found in some of Qatar's most opulent restaurants in addition to some of the country's most well-known street food establishments.

Therefore, if you're planning a trip to explore the attractions with your loved ones, be sure to sample Pani Puri wherever you find it since this is a dish from Qatar's street cuisine that you definitely shouldn't miss.

Regag / Crepe

Crepe, also known as Ragag, is a delectable Arabic street snack that is very well-liked by both residents and visitors in Qatar.

Although it may not be the greatest meal in Qatar, this dish has all the makings of a well-liked street snack there. In reality, the majority of cafés and food stands in Qatar provide crepe to visitors.

A cone-shaped snack that is paper thin and often crunchy is folded or rolled. It goes well with tea, kebabs, cheese, eggs, and many other toppings. To improve the taste of the food, locals in Qatar also like to apply honey or thick fish paste on the crepe.

Khaboos

Have you ever enjoyed a meal made using flatbread in the Middle East or elsewhere? Khaboos is a popular dish among tourists to the Middle East that can be found on the streets of Doha. It is a cuisine that incorporates tastes from the Indian subcontinent. Maida is one of the key components, which makes it even more delectable as a snack. Khaboos may be consumed with hummus or dips. Only in the historic market known as Souq Waqif may one treat oneself to Khaboos.

Popcorn

Have you ever considered the flavor of popcorn in the Middle East? It's not similar to the ones that people often consume in Asia or any other region? Or maybe it is. Before the taste buds receive delight from the food, no one will ever know.

Popcorn, one of the world's most delectable foods, has recently established a presence in Qatar. It is the one food that is often consumed while watching a film or other series. It is claimed to be the preferred snack and can be seen on Qatari streets. Therefore, you truly have no clue what you're missing out on if you haven't treated yourself to some Middle Eastern popcorn.

So while exploring Qatar's streets, grab a bucket of popcorn and settle down. It is one of the numerous elements that contribute to a wonderful vacation.

The harees
A dish called harees or harissa is cooked with meat and pounded wheat that has been boiled and cracked. It has a texture that is a cross between porridge and dumplings. You should not worry if you are unsure about the flavor or if it will be healthy for your health. It is often consumed for breakfast during Iftar during Ramadan since it tastes delicious and provides a significant amount of nutrients.

These foods have a distinct flavor that is exclusive to the Middle East. People should pamper their taste senses to the greatest when on vacation since it is unlike any other food.

Kebab

Kebabs are among the most delectable delicacies that visitors to Qatar must experience. Kebab is a grilled beef meal with vegetables or other components that is drenched in fragrant spices. To entice your taste buds, it is grilled and served with a variety of bread and salads. It is a well-known Middle Eastern dish cooked over a fire that is also referred to as kofta. The aroma of the kebabs varies depending on whether they are baked in a pan or cooked on a skewer. It is the best street food in Qatar that you just can't pass up and will undoubtedly make your day.

Balaleet

Balaleet, which has a calming flavor, balances sweet and savory ingredients. In Qatar, this traditional meal is a favorite. Vermicelli, cardamom, sugar, rosewater, and even saffron combine to create the mouthwatering flavor of this Arabian treat. Regardless of your preference for sweets, you must taste this Qatari cuisine. It is one of the most well-liked breakfast options.

Qatar's World Cup drinking regulations?

Alcohol use is not permitted in Islam. As a consequence, it wasn't often consumed in the country.

But Qatar already has certain private clubs and high-end hotels that sell alcohol.

There will still be zero tolerance for drinking in public areas like the street during the World Cup. Alcohol will, however, be sold in some stadium areas and FIFA fan zones.

Fan zones for the Club World Cup 2019 in Qatar offered alcohol, with a drink costing £5.

Drinking in public is against the law in Qatar, according to the most recent UK government regulations. And those who consume alcohol in public places face fines or jail time of up to six months.

Chapter 5:TRANSPORTATION SYSTEMS
IN QATAR

More than 760 miles (1,230 km) of Qatar's
roads are paved, almost entirely. No
railways exist. The nation is home to several
significant ports, notably those at Doha and
Umm Sa'd. Doha has an international
airport, and Qatar Airways is the country's
flag carrier.

Doha Public Transportation
Because of the size of the nation and the
quality of the roads, traveling throughout
Qatar is not too difficult. Although driving is
the preferred mode of transportation in
Qatar, public transportation has
significantly improved recently, partly as a

result of the growth of its bus and metro services.

The majority of roadways in Qatar run to and from Doha, the country's capital, where visitors will arrive at Hamad International Airport. By automobile, it just takes a few hours to get through the nation. Take caution while driving since the roads may get busy.

Many visitors choose to travel to Qatar by taxi or hired a limousine because it's a highly handy (but pricey) option. To choose which choice best fits your budget, see our guide to public transportation in and around Doha.

Taxi

For short distances and excursions beyond the city, taxis may be booked (for a surcharge). The government-owned transportation firm Mowasalat runs Karwa

Taxi. In addition to having the largest fleet of vehicles, it is the only taxi company authorized to run at Hamad International Airport. Uber and Careem cabs, which operate through an app, are additional services.

Taxi prices in Doha are metered, starting at a minimum of 10 riyals and increasing by 1.6 or 1.9 riyals every kilometer depending on the time of day. Taxis are available at practically all hotels and retail centers, as well as at roadside cab stands. Call Karwa toll-free at 800-Cab (8294) or +974 4458 8888 if you aren't using a taxi app (an extra charge of 4 riyals levied).
edited Lawrence Wang picture (CC BY-SA 2.0)

2 Limo service

Although more costly than taxis, chauffeured limousine service in Qatar is the best option for tourists who want the ease of having a driver while on vacation. Depending on the passenger's requirements—whether they want a normal limo service, a bigger vehicle for groups, or a VIP ride—price ranges apply. Limousines may be hired at an hourly or daily rate.

In Qatar, you may choose from several limousine providers, including the government-run Mowasalat transportation service. Call 800-LIMO (5466) or 800-TAXI to reserve an Impala, Passat, Audi, or Mercedes Vito (7-seater) from Mowasalat (8294). The Karwa taxi application also allows for the reservation of limousines.

3 Car rental

In Qatar, renting a car is a reasonably priced form of transportation. There are several operators at Doha's international airport, or you may reserve a vehicle by contacting ahead or doing so online. International companies like Hertz and AVIS, as well as regional rental companies, provide car rental services.

Foreign drivers must provide their passports and either has an international driving permit or a license from a GCC (Gulf Cooperation Council) nation while renting a vehicle in Qatar.

4\sBus

A contemporary, air-conditioned public bus is operated by the Mowasalat transportation company on many routes from Hamad International Airport across Doha and all of Qatar.

Doha is connected by bus to the northern municipalities of Al Shamal, Umm Salal, and Al Khor, the western municipality of Dukhan City, and the southern communities of Abu Samra and Mesaieed City. For travel within Doha, fares begin at 3 riyals, while for travel outside of the city, they begin at 4 riyals. Daily bus service typically runs from 4 am until 11 night.

Before traveling, passengers must purchase a Karwa smartcard, which is sold at airport vending machines, the Pearl Qatar, the Doha Bus Station, and several other retail locations. For further information about bus schedules and participating Karwa card businesses, see the Mowasalat website.

Options for bus smartcards include a refillable Classic Card (30 riyals), a Limited Card (10 riyals) for up to two trips within 24 hours, and an Unlimited Card (50 riyals) for as many trips as desired within 24 hours (20 riyals). A fee of 10 riyals will be assessed to passengers who board without their smart cards.

The West Bay shuttle service in Doha is a well-liked route for tourists in Qatar. It connects West Bay to several attractions, such as the city center, the Corniche, and Al

Bidda Street. From 6 AM until 12 AM, shuttle buses operate every 15 minutes.

You may take advantage of day outings on private buses with Qatar Airways, including the Doha City Tour, Desert Tours, and a Stop-and-Shop Tour.

Metro

One of the most recent modes of public transportation in Qatar is the Doha Metro. The Red, Green, Gold, and Blue lines total over 300 kilometers in length and include 100 stops.

A trip card must be purchased by each user to utilize the Doha Metro. There are three different kinds: A paper card with limited use costs around 2 riyals and is good for only one trip. The Gold Travel Card is a reusable plastic card that costs around 100 riyals, whereas the Standard Travel Card is a reusable plastic card that costs about 10 riyals and does not provide access to the Gold Line.

The Yellow Line
The Red Line has 17 stops along its 40 km route from Al Wakra in the north to Lusail, including West Bay QIC, Katara, and Qatar University. Additionally, this route links Terminal 1 of Hamad International Airport with Qatar's city center.

The Yellow Line
Between Al Mansoura and Al Riffa, the Green Line travels from east to west. There are 11 stations along the route, featuring popular destinations such as the Qatar National Library, Al Shaqab, and Hamad Hospital.

Golden Line

From Ras Bu Abboud to Al Aziziyah, there are 11 stops along the east-west Gold Line. Among the important destinations along the Gold Line are the Qatar National Museum and Souq Waqif.

A blue line
The second phase of the metro's construction is represented by this fourth line.

Tram
A comprehensive national transportation strategy includes tram lines in West Bay and Lusail in addition to the Doha Metro service. The Lusail Tram will include 4 lines and 25 total stops, both above and below ground. It will serve as Lusail City's primary transportation hub, which is situated around 23 kilometers north of Doha.

Security

Males 18 years of age and older may choose not to serve in the military. Approximately 12,000 people, most of whom are in the army, make up Qatar's modest defense force, and the nation relies on its friends and neighbors to defend itself from any outside threats. However, the nation's military spending as a proportion of GDP is high—five times the global average and more than that of practically any other nation.

Chapter 6: FOR THE LOVE OF FOOTBALL

Qatar and the ticket to host the FIFA 2022 world cup

The World Cup in Qatar takes place later this year from 21 November to 18 December. It is set to be a tournament like no other as the host country has faced intense scrutiny in the build-up to the competition. The bidding process for Qatar has been subject to corruption investigations, while the nation has been criticised over worker abuses.

The Athletic has put together a guide to all the key bits of information around the World Cup.

Why is the Qatar World Cup taking place in the winter?

When Qatar won their bid in 2010, this year's World Cup was initially planned to take place in the summer in line with every previous tournament.

But with Qatar's average summer temperatures ranging from 95-113 degrees Fahrenheit (35-45°C) the tournament was rescheduled to take place in the winter months amid player and fan health concerns. That decision will cause issues for domestic leagues like the Premier League as they will have to pause their season.
It will still not necessarily be cold in November and December as the temperatures are still expected to be around 75°F (23°C).

What is the full World Cup match table
Group A: Qatar, Ecuador, Senegal, Netherlands
Group B: England, Iran, USA, Wales

Group C: Argentina, Saudi Arabia, Mexico, Poland

Group D: France, Australia, Denmark, Tunisia

Group E: Spain, Costa Rica, Germany, Japan

Group F: Belgium, Canada, Morocco, Croatia

Group G: Brazil, Serbia, Switzerland, Cameroon

Group H: Portugal, Ghana, Uruguay, South Korea

World Cup Stadiums in Qatar 2022

The 2022 FIFA World Cup will not only be the first tournament to be held in the Arab region, but it will be the most compact, allowing fans to attend more than one game a day.

With high summer temperatures, each stadium, training facility and fan zone is equipped with solar-powered cooling technology to keep the temperature at 27C. All stadiums are eco-friendly and their temperature will be controllable.

Al Bayt Stadium
Host city: Al Khor
Gross capacity: 60,000
Matches planned: Opening game and all matches through to the semi-finals
Delivered by Aspire Zone Foundation, this stadium can seat up to 60,000 spectators. It is unique with its giant tent structure covering the whole stadium that is named after bayt al sha'ar – tents historically used by nomadic peoples in Qatar and the Gulf region.

The stadium's design honors Qatar's past and present while being a model of green development and sustainability. After the tournament, the upper part of the stadium will be dissembled and the removed seats will be donated to other countries.

Ahmad Bin Ali Stadium
Host city: Al Rayyan
Gross capacity: 40,000

Matches planned: Group   matches, round of 16
Located in Al Rayyan just outside of Doha, Al-Rayyan Stadium will expand to hold 40,000 spectators using modular elements forming an upper tier in time for the 2022 FIFA World Cup.

The stadium is reflecting the Qatari culture through its "spectacular undulating façade". It will be downsized to nearly 20,000 seats after the tournament, and the removed seats

will be given to football development
projects abroad.

Al Janoub Stadium
Host city: Al Wakrah
Gross capacity: 40,000

Matches planned: Group matches and
round of 16
Located in Al Wakrah, 18 kilometers away
from Doha, this stadium has a capacity of
40,000, and is part of a broader sports
complex that contains cycling and horse
trails, shops, restaurants and sports clubs.
After the FIFA World Cup, the stadium's
capacity will be reduced to 20,000 seats,
guaranteeing an electric atmosphere for
their Qatar Stars League matches.

Khalifa International Stadium
Host city: Doha
Gross capacity: 40,000

Matches planned: Group   matches, round of 16, and play off for third place game

The redesigned Khalifa International Stadium was originally built in 1976 and renovated and expanded in 2005 to serve as the centerpiece of the 2006 Asian Games hosted by Qatar.

The stadium, which includes sweeping arcs and partially covered stands, is the centerpiece of Aspire Zone, a sports complex that includes Aspire Academy for Sports Excellence, Hamad Aquatic Centre, ASPETAR Sports Medicine Hospital and many other sporting venues.

Attached to the stadium via a walkway is the 3-2-1 Qatar Olympic and Sports Museum, adding to the appreciation of how this venue cherishes its past as it builds towards an exciting future.

Qatar Foundation Stadium

Host city: Al Rayyan (Education City)
Gross capacity: 40,000
Matches planned: Group   matches, round of 16, and and quarter-finals
The new Education City Stadium is located in the midst of several world-class university campuses at Qatar's global center of excellence, Education City.

The stadium can seat up to 40,000 spectators, and it takes the form of a jagged diamond. It is easily accessible for fans by either road or metro. Following the FIFA World Cup, the stadium will retain 25,000 seats for use by university athletic teams.

For decades to come, Qatar Foundation Stadium will be a symbol of innovation, sustainability and progress, in line with Qatar National Vision 2030 and the goals of both Qatar Foundation and the Supreme Committee for Delivery & Legacy.

Lusail Stadium

Host city: Lusail
Gross capacity: 80,000
Matches planned: All matches through to the final match
Located in Al Daayen section which is part of the developed Lusail City, the new Lusail Stadium is one of the primary stadiums of Qatar's World Cup and will host the final ceremony for the 2022 tournament.

Fans will get to games via upgraded roads, the Doha Metro or the Lusail Light Rail Transit system, and they can spend their time across different parks or in the theme park.

Ras Abu Aboud Stadium
Host city: Doha
Gross capacity: 40,000
Matches planned: Group matches and round of 16
Ras Abu Aboud stadium project is a pioneering project in the world of sports stadium construction. Built from shipping

containers, this stadium will be completely dismantled and the materials that were used in the construction will be re-utilized.

The stadium is located minutes away from Hamad International Airport and it overlooks the Gulf Coast and the fascinating scene of the West Bay skyscrapers.

Al Thumama Stadium
Host city: Doha
Gross capacity: 40,000
Matches planned: Group   matches, round of 16, and quarter finals
Al Thumama Stadium is a distinct Arab architectural icon, as it is inspired by the traditional qahfiya (the cap worn under the Ghutra and Egal) in the Arab world. This design was chosen because it is a cultural commonality among Arabs in the Arab world. Therefore, it expresses the Arab civilization's depth and the intertwined

cultural-historical legacy of the Arab countries.

The stadium is located in the southern districts of Doha, several minutes away from Hamad International Airport, and has a capacity of at least 40,000 seats that will be reduced after the tournament to 20,000 and donated to developing countries.

Made in the USA
Middletown, DE
24 October 2022

13386005R00053